Your True Name

Poems, Songs, and Stories
to find your way to you.

Bobby Jo Valentine

Doodles by Thomas Kinsfather

Table of Contents

Introduction

My True Name

I've been discovering my true name my whole life. I believe most of us do. We pick up clues along the way and lose the plot from time to time. But deep inside, we long for a grounding, core identity, a feeling of knowing our unique set of loves, dislikes, wishes, fears, and dreams.

Two days after I was born, I was adopted into a loving family with a strong religious core. Early on, I understood there were two Bobby's: the natural born Bobby and the Bobby that I "should be".

The first Bobby was bright and wild, with a fierce imagination and a love of both the outer and inner landscape. My True Name. My favorite game was Make Believe. I would go into the backyard and lose myself (and my friends) in worlds unseen. I loved books, and the librarian at my local library kept busy piling my arms full of ones that would unlock my imagination. I grew a constant wonder about what the world could be, and what I could become.

The second Bobby was a collection of expectations that my school, my family, and friends had of me. The good Christian ideal was to be an upstanding member of my family, and a well-adjusted Baptist boy. This was the "name" I found myself trying, and often failing, to measure up to. This identity was often in contrast to the one that I innately held inside of me.

If I wanted to fit better as Bobby #2 – the one that people wanted me to be– then I'd need to subjugate my natural behaviors. I had to dream less and memorize/recite more. I had to keep an eye and ear out for social cues and then pattern myself to match. I had to act, talk, and become more like the good Baptist boy that was requested or required of me.

Almost everyone goes through the process of trading in our soul's true self for the identity that the system requires of you. And it starts early, while you're still putting yourself together. Because you're being told who you should be, there's less room to discover who you are. And before you know it, you become only a fraction of yourself, with dozens of "identity add-ons" that are harder and harder to shed as time goes on.

It took me 22 years for the big turning point to start getting my True Name back. I came to terms with the fact that I was gay. No amount of praying would take it away. It was a core piece of my identity. Choosing to be honest about this meant walking away from the name I'd built on the expectations of others. Slowly but surely, I started getting back to other key pieces of my identity – that I loved to write, I loved to sing, and that the art I created had a knack for connecting people to their deeper selves.

As I understand it, our True Name is the deep, soft, strong voice constantly calling us into honest action. It knows what will give us purpose, bring us joy, and the gifts we've been given that can make the world a better place. It is the spiritual, soul-centering affirmation that we belong here, just as we are, and that being ourselves is the best way to belong.

Rediscovering and living into our True Name is a lifelong process. It isn't a straight line. Every business is trying to tie our personal worth to their product or service, pulling us towards their definition of satisfaction and truth. Also, most careers come with some sort of compromise to our truest way of moving through the world. There are a thousand false paths, with the best billboards and salesmen, pulling us away from our essential selves dozens of times a day.

With these songs, poems and stories, I hope to offer a path home to your own True Name. They come from my own journey to find what is deeply real about my life and the universe. The discovery from hundreds of concerts is that the closer I write and sing from my own core, the more I tap into what is inside all of us. We all long for a sense of home. We all have dreams that invite us to greater and deeper meaning-making. We all need to be opened from the inside, in the way only love can do.

My True Name, for me, is called forth whenever my inner spirit resonates with anything – a song, an experience, a person, or a poem. When I sense that hum of "Yes, this is beautiful to me. Yes, this is true for me," I get inspired to let go of the false identities others have given me or that I've given myself.

There are all sorts of ways to read a book of poetry. For this one, I invite you to read it all the way through at your own pace, and then perhaps read one twice a day - upon waking and right before bed – so the soul medicine might do its work. Many of them started as songs, so the 'meter' will be different then a typical poem, and some of them still have a chorus that repeats - but hopefully they still "work".

My wish is that somewhere along this book, the words here speak your True Name. Just like swallowing a pill heals you from the inside out, it's my dream that some words you read travel deep inside and give medicine to anything good and true that's been lost, hurt, or hidden. That they call you out of hiding to live fully into your life. I know that's an ambitious hope, but if you know me, you know dreaming big is part of my own True Name. Thank you so much for reading.

Hearts

Hopeful Terrain

It is amazing how much words can affect a heart. Especially a young heart.

I grew up attending a small Baptist school from Kindergarten through 12th grade with a total of about 75 kids. Long before I knew what sexuality was, I knew I was different. I preferred keeping to myself or being with one friend at a time. I loved getting alone in a corner and burying my face in a book or a video game. And with being different, comes what happens when other kids realize you're different – annoyance, insult, bullying. By the time I got to Junior High, I was the easiest target in school for pranks, for name-calling, for being told I was something less than normal.

Some of this definitely motivated me to get through school as quickly as possible. Tthe entire school was based on ACE (Accelerated Christian Education) self-paced curriculum, and I barreled through. I graduated from high school before Christmas break, when I was 16. Then, right after turning 17, I went off to West Coast Baptist College and became "the perfect Baptist."

I carried the bullying names with me far into adulthood, fighting against the false identities heaped on me by other people. I was called quite a list of untrue names. Even today, I can find myself surprised at the names my mind calls me. When I dig deeper, I find it's an old voice from long ago, full of fear and ignorance and menace.

The more I get to know my true self – the one capable of loving almost everyone, hopeful to a fault, and lovable – the easier I'm able to spot an old false label, and the faster I'm able to trade it in for the truth. But some wounds go deep down into the innermost circle of your identity.

How can we heal the deepest wound of our heart? We have no chance unless we are willing to get to know the terrain.

Strong Enough

Be careful the doors that you open
With the words that you speak
And the people who will hold them
'Cause long ago, someone told me I was broken and it stuck

I've tried to pull the words away
But my hands are never strong enough

Have you ever read a shadow sentence
That filled your spirit with shame
People can call you by so many things
That aren't your true name
And yes, we all get angry
And yes, we all get tired
But just remember what leaves your mouth
Can fuel or fade someone else's fire

Know when a hurting soul hurts you
They're only passing their pain
They probably don't know your story
And they don't know your true name
That you are loved and forgiven
That you are good at your core
That you are stronger now because of
The shadowlands you walked through before

So be careful the doors that you open
With the words that you speak
And the people who will hold them
Cause long ago, someone told me I was broken and it stuck

I've tried to pull the words away
But my hands are never strong enough

But I know my True Name
I know my True Name.
Long ago, someone told me I was broken
But I know my True Name.
People can call you by so many things
But I know my True Name.

Shades of Color

I am far more happy
then you ever notice
I am far more sad
then I will ever show
I am both of these
and more inside each moment
I am shades of color
you may never know

The Thing About A Heart

I was at a protest in Seattle one day
All the cool kids had so much to say
I think there's certainly a time and a place
To let out all your anger and pain
But then I turned on the news after work
And everyone there was still speaking hurt
Fighting over who did and didn't deserve
The things we humans go through each day

And I don't think that anyone's mind has been changed
Using shame or anger or pride
Because the thing about a heart is it opens from the inside.

Both of my parents vote much differently then I do
I'm sure there's lots of big things we could fight through
But they're getting older now, so most these days I choose
To join them for walks in the park
We move our bodies through the bushes and trees
And stop to point out a bird we haven't seen
Sometimes I think this might be all that we need
Love doesn't have to be hard

But either way I know, If i yelled at them both
We'd go back to our corners and hide
Because the thing about a heart is it opens from the inside.

I flipped the channels on my noisy TV
Trying to find myself some sense of relief
From all the faces that were shouting on screen
Fighting for their viewers to stay
Then, I stumbled on a quiet scene at a lake
At first I thought I'd hit the mute by mistake
There wasn't anyone to bill or to blame
Just the sense the Earth was doing okay

So I imagined all the newscasters there
Water in their eyes, wind in their hair
Nobody saying what was fair or unfair,
Nothing to get in the way

And then all at once
In my dream
They all realize
That the thing about a heart is it opens from the inside.
From the inside.

My Border

Welcome to my border.

Please step across
Let's sit a while.

When I was 5 years old
There was no border.
And I, the Statue of Liberty.

Whoever sailed to my shores
Got through.
Huddled masses, tempest tossed
I loved them all

And then.
Well, you can see the chain link fence.
I got afraid.
I got suspicious.

Here, have a drink.
Anyway...my border.

I cross it sometimes
To invite a friend
But if they step over
Usually it is short lived.

I wait for an infraction
And as soon as it happens
My torch of freedom burns

And the ones who came for safety
Become tempest-tossed again.

If you see, over there
I have started to build a wall

It might take some of my work,
some of my self

But I believe, in time,
I will either make
Or become it.

Slow Down, Feel It

Tony the tiger doesn't live here anymore
He turned tail, he left town, trying to settle some score,
He got a one way ticket and a traveling case
He doesn't do anything half-way

Some say the circus wasn't paying enough
Some say the money was so good
he started feeling out of touch,
Some say his love started to feel like a crutch
So Tony had to find his own way

From plane to train, from town to town
He picked up almost as soon as he touched down
A voice playing in the back of his mind
He tried to ignore kept popping up from time to time

Slow down, feel it
Unless you let it hurt you're never gonna heal it
Slow down, slow down, slow down…feel it

So I wake up and take my things off the floor
Hope I can figure out what all this leaving is for,
I hope the bridges I burn I can return to someday
But I don't do anything half-way

From plane to train, from town to town
I pick up almost as soon as I touch down
A voice somewhere in the back of my mind
I've try to ignore keeps popping up from time to time

Slow down, feel it
Unless you let it hurt you're never gonna heal it

So I stop by and lay some roses on the door
No flowers ever will settle this score,
I got a one way ticket and a traveling case
I have to find my own way

Drive past the city, til everything glistens
Pull over, stop, and finally start to listen
My ground of being, my significant other
Rises up inside me, both father and mother and says

Slow Down, feel it
Unless you let it hurt you're never going to heal it
Slow down, slow down, slow down…feel it

All the Love

When life starts to lose its color
In the blurring and the busy
May you find in loving others
All the love that you've been missing

There's a sister and a brother
Who are lost, barely existing
And they need you to recover
All the love that you've been missing

Chase Away My Dark

Four walls I built of tin
Out past the city, stars and freedom
I can't let my feelings in
Cause I would not know where to lead them
Plus that would mean I need them
And that would be too hard
I need some love to chase away my dark

I broke my heart before
I know it hurts, no need to show me
It's been years since I left this shore
I hear the sirens getting lonely
But I don't want them to know me
I've got too many scars
I need some love to chase away my dark

So far this sinking ship
Feels like it's past the point of leaving
Too scared to take the trip
To out where the loved and lost are leaving
But the heart is prone to beating
And souls aren't meant to starve
So I need some love to chase away my dark

Not A Fire Escape

I've seen those fading eyes before, the dim light of a closing door
I know you need another core to ground you
So I let down my deep defense, and despite all the evidence
I wrap my wounded, weathered fence around you

I'm here, dry your face, this is not the time to count up our mistakes
I'm here, for now, but then you ask if love could hurt a little less somehow

Oh no, wait a minute
Who told you
Love wouldn't cost you a thing?
Love is a fire and nothing burns for free,

Hold on, who told you
Love's not a risk that we take
Love is a fire, not a fire escape
So burn me up

It's easy not to light a fuse, you don't know if the heart you choose
Will hurt or heal or comfort or confound you
But I've been through Love's darker side
So I'll carry your weight and mine
And wrap my wounded, weathered light around you
I'm here, dry your eyes, this is not the time for leaving or goodbyes
I'm here, for now, but if you ask if love could hurt a little less somehow

Who told you
Love doesn't cost you a thing?
Love is a fire and nothing burns for free.
Who told you
Love's not a risk that we take?
Love is a fire, not a fire escape
So burn me up

The Last Resort

Don't save love for the last resort
That's not what it's for
It's the first line of the play
It's the first thing you should say

So much waiting, so little time
To say what's on your soul
So much praying for a sign
When you already know

There's a statue on a hill
Closed lips and cold eyes
Saying we should wait until
Evidence arrives

But don't save love for the last resort
That's not what it's for
Don't save love for the last resort
It's the first line of the play.

Hurts

Losing Your Pig

In 2021, a movie came out that moved me instantly to song. It was called "Pig."

In the film, Nicholas Cage plays a chef named Rob who abandoned his career in the city after the death of his wife. He combs the forest for truffles with the help of his pig, the only living thing he's still attached to. When his pig is kidnapped, he must go back into the city he left because of his deep pain and grief to find it. He comes back in touch with his past life and must face the truth of his wife's loss.

Well, SPOILER ALERT…

The pig dies. And there's a moment at the end of the film when Rob is talking to the young guy, Amir, who drove him through the city searching. Rob says that before finding out it was dead, it was as if the pig was still alive. The young man looks at Rob and says "But it wasn't alive. It's dead."

What a perfect picture of the human instinct to protect ourselves from pain by pretending it doesn't exist. This simple, blunt statement allows Rob to finally soften and attend to the wound of his wife's passing. The film ends with the first step to healing…turning towards, instead of away from, the hurt.

Jamie Anderson once said "Grief is just love with no place to go." I love that idea of love as a motion…a movement…that can become stuck when loss overwhelms us. Love calls us forward into life again, tough, and though it can't change our painful past, in time, if we're lucky and if we do the work, love can flow again to other people, other places. Eventually the story softens, the grace creeps in.

First, though, before we can heal…we must speak about what hurts. We must name it aloud, and allow it to speak back to us in turn. When we hear our pain's voice, when we really listen…we recognize it as what it almost always is. The ache for love, and to love.

Out In The Woods

Out in the woods
Back to the basics
Far from the world
Don't have to face it
Day after day
Learn the trees languages
Staying away from
The painful bright pavement

Living alone with what you've lost
Comes at a cost

Long, long ago
I lived to love others, but
One dealt a blow
I never recovered from
In a way, though
I still hear a chorus
Of joy and of play
In this cavernous forest:

Follow the love in your life
Don't be afraid of it
Follow the love in your life
And know you are made of it

Life threw me back
Into the city
Seeing how bad
My old pals were living
Most of them sold
Themselves to be playthings
Trading their soul
For status and savings

Trading a dream for what it costs
Comes at a loss, so
Follow the love in your life
Don't be afraid of it
Follow the love in your life
And know you are made of it

Out in the Woods
Back to the basics
The city is lost, but
I don't have to save it
I'm less a recluse now
More like a resident
A voice inside me
Is starting to speak again:

Follow the love in your life
Don't be afraid of it
Follow the love in your life
And know you are made of it.

Lost comes natural to me

As soon as my feet leave the ground
I'm chasing a brand new sound
So hard to stay happy while found
When lost comes natural to me

I've met a few wonderful men
Who said "Never leave home again"
But it's hard to see wandering's end
When lost comes natural to me

I've been to so many good towns
They loved me and said settle down
But hard to grow roots in the ground
When lost comes natural to me

Bones

Life is a table set for five and they're eating us alive in it
Life is a race we race one time and
we tend to drink and drive in it
And we travel any other path except the path that leads us home
We're breaking more than just our bones

All my fears come out at night and I do not forget to feed em
And I am in a constant fight between
my father's house and freedom
Feels like our only choices are the devil or the great unknown
We're breaking more than just our bones

And while I'm thankful for the arms
that have opened and received me
Still I can't fight off the faces of the ones who chose to leave me
And I travel any other path except the path that leads me home
We're breaking more than just our bones

Haunted House

I am a haunted house
And it's a quarter after three
And there are flashes of blue light
As my love of life fights
With the pain in me
I am a haunted house
And there are eyes behind my doors
You're gonna have to walk about
If you're going to figure out
What the fear is really for

See the markings on the cedars
Hear the footprints down the hall
There is someone in the window
There is no one there at all
I am a haunted house
And there are spirits in these posts
If you wanna come near,
You're going to have to clear it with the ghosts

I am a haunted house
And there are shadows in my seams
I see the sharp teeth of dark memories
Trying to feast upon my dreams
There's a picture on the shelf
Of a boy who's nearly ten
Behind him a warm red glow
Where somebody should have been

See the markings on the cedars
Read the writing on the wall
And the specters in the mirror
They don't look like me at all
I burn the candles slowly
There isn't much light left
What's dancing in the darkness
Has my defeat upon its breath

I am a haunted house
And there are spirits in these posts
If you wanna come near,
You're going to have to clear it with the ghosts

Shark

As scary movies go,
Jaws was my first
Shown to me, unguarded
6 years old
At my aunt's.

Opaque water
Rippling danger
Sharp surprise

And an idea, planted deep inside me:
The less you can see
The more it can hurt.

So began
My toxic relationship
With mystery

Real Love

No matter where I go
I always miss the sun
I'm always on the ropes
I'm always on the run
To me, it seems that love
It's always lost and found
It's such a winding road
And this is such a lonely town

Oh, I need real love
So I won't say never
But I'm scared of real love
They say nothing lasts forever

The past is all I own
And demons mark the tracks
Some memories I hold close
Some memories hold me back
I want to be seduced
To take the sunset slow
I want to be confused
To wander down this lonely road with someone else

Oh, I need real love
So I won't say never
But I'm scared of real love
They say nothing lasts forever
If you wanna come near,
You're going to have to clear it with the ghosts

Alone, Pt. 1

There's a subtle but striking
Difference in tone
Between lonely and only
Being alone

Alone, Pt. 2

Being alone
Is so different now
Because before, being lonely,
I didn't even have \
Myself.

Home

We drop like falling stars
Bare feet and cable cars
We don't know who we are
But we're not trying to find out
We stare up at the sun
Look at the things we've done
My heart is on the run
And it's not gonna stop now

Oh, but sometimes I want to go home.

We wear our doubts like skin
Look at the mess we're in
Somebody's gotta win
I'm not trying to win now

Oh, but sometimes I want to go home.

We wear our fear like scars
Scared that we've come this far
We don't know who we are
And we're afraid to find out

Oh, but sometimes
I want to go home.

Haunt Me Gently

If you're going to haunt me, haunt me gently
Slowly pull the covers off me
Whisper incantations softly
Keep your apparitions kind
If you're going to haunt me, do it nicely
Send me treasures to remind me
It's worthwhile to keep on going
Though you're always on my mind

I won't forget the day you left me…
But if you're going to haunt me,
Haunt me gently

Big Bad Choice

It almost felt like flying,
The day I started falling down
It was electrifying
Like what you feel before you drown

Or so I've heard, that's just pretense
A way to word my thoughts to make some sense
Anyways, that's all just noise
Back to the story of my big bad choice

Love was my main objective
And I thought there was something there
My friends were so protective
They saw me leave and they got scared
Or so I've heard
Down through the rumor mill
And they're just words,
But words can kill
Anyways, that's all just noise
Back to the story of my Big Bad Choice

8 months they said they loved me
8 months and 27 days
They seemed so high above me
But I still loved them anyway
And then one night
She said that it had been a lie
And I turned white
Tried to speak, found no voice
And that's the story of my Big Bad Choice
I heard my mother calling
I heard my father saying wait
But I was water falling
Into the rocks without delay
And I have heard
The greatest truth comes
When your heart runs out of words
But I am there,
And there's no noise
Except the echo of a big bad choice

It's Just a Phase

When I came out, the first thing that my Baptist superiors suggested was to go to a "reform program" – otherwise known as a conversion therapy center, where people help you go from gay to straight. I visited two camps. At the first one, the leader's selling point was, "Now, when I watch TV shows, I find myself attracted to women over men." What an incentive!

I was attending seminary at the time, and told the Dean, who had a degree in Psychology, that I was gay. He thought he could counsel the gay out of me with one counseling session a week. After weeks, we were both unable to answer the question: If being gay is a choice, why would I, growing up in a culture that hates homosexuality, want to choose the one thing that was the most hated activity? He had no answer and neither did I. Thankfully, around this time I found a man who loved me amid my struggle, and saved me from feeling I needed fixing.

Thirteen years later, my friend Sean asked me to write a song about conversion therapy for a musical about his own life. "It's just a phase" describes his extraordinarily difficult time at the camp he was forced to attend, and mirrors hundreds of queer stories of people who mean well, but because of their beliefs, ask us to deny our love's deepest desire and direction.

It's just a phase

It's just a phase
That's what they say
We have a way to make the feelings go away
That rush of heat
When he walks by
We have a way to dull the twinkle in his eye
It's just a phase
This love you feel
We have a way of making rainbows look less real

Give it some time, you'll be okay
It's just a phase

It's just a phase,
we have the proof
Here is the story of a boy who looks like you
He took our path, believed our words
Gave up some happiness but it could be much worse
He could have let his heart fly free
Could you imagine all the places he could be

Instead of here, making our case
That it's just a phase

Just come inside and shut the door
We've helped so many people lose a love like yours
We'll make the romance run away
If you get lonely, all you have to do is pray

It's just a phase, you'll be alright
We have a way of making rainbows black and white

Give it some time, you'll be okay
It's just a phase.

You Are Too Nice

I was told
at twelve years old.

What a sacrilege

To believe in
"too much"
kindness.

What a weight
Upon my shoulders

This control
Over my goodness.

How long
It took
To break
That grip.

Hope

The Beauty Underneath

In 2017, a fire burned through Napa County, California where I lived with my partner. I was on tour in Kansas City at the time, and at 1am we got the call from his son that the flames were getting close to our house. We stayed up for 3 hours in limbo before the firefighters made his son evacuate. We got on the earliest flight home, and when we landed, so did a text from his son...the house had been completely burned to the ground, along with everything in it.

In the weeks and months that followed, we tried to piece our life back together. The kindness of our support group brought instruments, sound equipment, and clothes back into our lives, but John had lost priceless antiques that had belonged to his family for generations, and I'd lost every keepsake that carried any significance. It was unspeakably hard.

It took me months before I felt emotionally stable enough to drive back to the site of the fire. The road to the house wound up a hillside, and as I rounded the last turn, I was afraid of what I was going to see.

But instead of a burnt house, because it was completely gone, I was greeted with the most beautiful view of the Napa Valley. Sweeping green, under a lush blue sky. It was a reminder that, even with everything we'd lost, there was still so much beauty in the world.

In that moment, a choice became clear: to travel through life looking at what's lost, or looking at what's left.

I've always loved foxes. It is amazing how, when we hike through a forest, we can see a big boulder or fallen tree and think nothing of it. But to a fox, that can mean the world - shelter, protection, a place to raise their children. They would look underneath the boulder and see something greater than we would. Hope is like that. It looks for the beauty underneath the darkest, the difficult, the most mundane. Hope is the whisper that says "Life is more than the ache, the doldrums, the depression, the chaos you feel right now. Look further. Go deeper. You will get through this. Yes, even this. And look at what's still here. So much beauty."

Fox Eyes

Rooster crows at dawn
Hibernate instead
Deer eyes on the head lights up ahead
Migrate with the herd
Circle round the sun
Hope that all the groundhog days are done

What to do when all the reasons have worn thin
After all, we're only
Human animals with fur and souls and skin

Well, keep your fox eyes focused
On the beauty underneath
And keep your whale heart open
That is all you really need to love life

Teeth and blood and sweat and tears
Tell me what it's worth
Temporary paw prints on this earth

What's the reason not to stay inside the shell
After all, we're only
Human animals with limbs and souls and cells

Well, keep your fox eyes focused
There is beauty underneath
And keep your whale heart open
That is all you really need to love life.

When they don't love you anymore
When your own story is the only left worth fighting for
When no one's opening the door
When the wolves come out at night
When there's no one left in sight
Are we going to be alright?

Well, keep your fox eyes focused
There is beauty underneath
And keep your whale heart open
That is all you really need to love life.

Fly

this is my room and it's robin's egg blue and it's got a few cracks
in the ceiling
this is my street where the minute-men meet and dad says that
i'll never be leaving
i'm ten years old but i know how to smoke and the drinks help
to cure the bad feelings
this is my home and the sticks and the stones
are made up of the darkest of things

but in my dreams i can fly and i soar and my feet touch the sky
it seems i can go anywhere if i try
and the world's not so dark when the clouds make it white
if there's no hope, tell me why
in my dreams i can fly

here come the tears and i cover my ears and i swear i can hear
my own heart-beat
when they stop fighting to turn out the lights i pretend that I'm
already sleeping
after the violence Alone in the silence just me and the secret I'm
keeping
my dad tells me i'm not worth anything and i've almost
admitted defeat

but in my dreams I can fly and i soar and my feet touch the sky
and it seems i can go anywhere if i try
and the world's not so dark when the clouds make it white
if there's no hope, tell me why
in my dreams i can fly

A Larger Life After All

Every Island is an iceberg of sorts
Beneath the floating illusion
Of separateness,
It is knit to everything else
All the way connected
Its hidden family tied together
By the ocean floor

When isolated or isolating,
Any of us on the surface level
Seem to stand apart
But, submerged in life's sea,
We are still cradled underneath
By a matrix of conversations and care
Stretching back
Into almost ancestral infinity

Telling us, if we ever feel
We have lost touch
Or feel adrift,
To just go deeper
Until we find ourselves tethered to
A Larger Life after all

Find the Light

I was sitting by a window
On a lazy afternoon
The brilliant sun was beaming
Through the trees into my room
My mind was spinning circles
Through some dark, difficult dreams
When a sudden dash of color
Splashed right through my reckonings
I don't know how it came to me
It hit me by surprise
Seven colors, all transparent
Right in front of my sad eyes

Every moment has a rainbow
If you only make it shine
If you find the perfect angle
You'll discover the Divine.
When your look on life starts fading
Into gray and black and white,
There's a rainbow in each moment
If you only find the light

Scared of Being Born

I think you're scared of being born
I've seen you hiding from the burning sun
I've seen your rivers, how their branches run
Away from any larger sea
I think you're scared of coming out
I've seen you looking at the door with doubt
How every chance you get to choose your way
You never choose mystery

Do you see darkness in each dare
Or think wings don't repair if they get torn
I don't think death is why you're scared
I think you're scared of being born

I think you're scared of breaking free
I know how comfortable a chain can be
When it's tied to friends and family
And old, familiar ghosts
I think you're scared to move away
Your life says to go but all your locks say stay
Just stay right here and throw the keys away
Keep your kin and comforts close

Do you think you can't try again
Or that pieces won't mend if they get torn,
I don't think death is why you're scared
I think you're scared of being born

Temporary Weather

This is my new room
This is my new room, and there's no one here
To help me break through, to make it all clear
Just a little pain
Like a little rain on my rooftop
Thought that it would drain
But instead it stops
And pools above my rib cage

Bringing me down with the temperature
Making me wonder why these shifts
Always feel like diseases, never a cure

Hold it together, I don't know whether
Or not we'll make it change is scary
Hold it together, maybe this weather
Is temporary, maybe a change will come soon

So this is my new plan
Do the best I can with the pieces left
Steady hands, deep, deep breath
Just a little doubt
Like a little cloud on my rooftop
Thought it would fade out but instead it stops
And stays beneath my shoulder blades

Clouding me up with the temperature
Making me wonder why the future
Always feels misty, there's nothing for sure

What's this? just a little sun
On the damage done to my rooftop
Thought it would never come
But it warms the place above my rib cage

Raising me up with its temperature
Filling me up with a sense
That life can be trusted, pain has a cure

So hold it together, I don't know whether
Or not we'll make it change is scary
But hold it together, I know that weather is temporary
I know a change will come soon.

Daisy

Daisy lifts her face towards the sun
Greets it with a kiss, takes it for a run
I hope I'm more like Daisy by the time my days are done

Daisy treats the day like it's alive
Feeds it with her love, listens to it sigh
And if it goes downhill, she just gives it another try

Daisy keeps her head out of the clouds
Lets her heart stay here, in the magic now
I hope I'm more like Daisy when tomorrow comes somehow

Daisy laughs as much as Daisy can
Mouth wide in delight, chest clutched in her hands
Daisy knows the best jokes aren't that hard to understand

Daisy lets the grief pass through and be
Doesn't try to change, force it to go free
Daisy knows that sadness is love with nowhere to be

So Daisy lifts her face towards the sky
Thanks it for the day, kisses it goodbye
I hope I'm more like Daisy every day until I die

A Place to Belong

Well I have watched thousands of sunsets
And seen the moon dissolve and resurrect
And I have slept in hundreds of bedrooms
But never once woke up at home.

But I believe that there is a place
Where my heart can breath,
A place where I can be happy
And so I keep searching
For that land wherever I go

But all I've got are broken guitar strings,
To help me sing my broken songs,
And even though I feel I've seen everything
I still haven't found a place to belong

I have walked through forests and canyons
I have prayed at hundreds of altars
Raised my hands at crystal cathedrals
And never once heard God speak.

But I believe that there is a hand
That is holding me as I walk this land
And it's guiding me, and it understands
And it carries me when I am weak

But there might be something wrong with me,
There might be something wrong
Cause even though I feel I've seen everything
I still haven't found a place to belong

Belly of the Beast

A man is selling fables
Like he has always done before
Something scrapes on a table
Someone is settling a score
And I don't know how i found you
There must be millions here at least
But i wrap my arms around you
Deep in the belly of the beast

It's so easy to enter
A Serengeti state of mind
One day you are Adventure
The next you're always out of time
First life breaks down and bleeds you
Then offers you a hollow feast
And then the hunger feeds you
Into the belly of the beast

I think a kind hand leads you
I think you're going to be alright
You take the time you need to
I will stay on the phone all night
All i can do is listen
And try to speak the words you need
But every voice feels distant
From in the belly of the beast

Don't think you're less than others
Because you're wounded from the war
Friend, you have many brothers
We've been there many times before
And i don't know how it saved me
But love crept in and made a key
And it will lead you safely
Out the belly of this beast

The New Medusa

Here comes the new Medusa
Snakes on the TV screen tonight
All hail the new Medusa
So hard to look away when fear catches your eye

Suspicion almost steals our humanity
A new apocalyptic soul calamity

Let's be strong, won't be long
It's going to take some time
Before right comes from the wrong
But trust the song

Let's be strong, won't be long
It's going to take some time
Before the minor chord resolves
Trust the song

Fear starts as a solo siren
How quick the violent virus grows
So we try to become islands
But even islands aren't alone
As every siren knows

Suspicion almost steals our humanity
Instead I'm treating every face like family

Hold on, let's be strong
It's going to take some time
Before the minor chord resolves
Trust the song

Helps

The Helpers

I have bipolar disorder.

It's shown up in many forms. One is depression, the worst episode lasting over 9 months, the majority of which I spent in bed, pretending I was fine to all my friends and trying (and failing) to sleep my life away. The other side is mania, a bright fiery euphoric state where your mind gets convinced of increasingly chaotic and destructive ideas that result in wild spending, terrible explosions of anger, and sometimes physical outbursts. Depression is extremely difficult, don't get me wrong, but mania to me is far worse because of how it affects the people around you. The hardest manic episode resulted in me hurting people I cared about the most, and a period of two months in jail. I'm grateful to say, coming out of that experience, that healing and reconciliation of nearly all relationships has happened, and people have responded with enormous kindness to my horrified, grief-stricken apologies and efforts to make amends.

Among the mental health issues people can have, bipolar is "notoriously difficult" to treat, according to Mellissa Suran, PHD. But it can be helped, through medication, therapy, and the love and support of good family and friends. In order to get through it and get to the balanced state I am today, I had to be willing to ask for help, and also to roll up my sleeves and do the work that only I could do.

In times of turmoil and trouble, Mr. Rogers would always say to "look for the helpers." After I was helped back to health, I wanted to be one of those helpers. Internal exploration, discovery, and healing are so important. The final reason for and result of inner work though, I feel, extends beyond our own feelings and state of mind. I want my mental health to allow me to help – to do good in the world, to be there for others, to create beauty and share my story in a way that inspires people. And I know, deep down, we all want the same - for our inner journeys to make a difference in the outside world, too.

There's no better feeling than knowing that help is on the way…except, perhaps, being that help for someone that needs it. That is a gift like no other. Now that I've found balance, I get messages from people struggling with mental health all over the world, asking for help, asking to be seen, asking for hope. It was life-saving for me to receive help – and now, it's so life-affirming to give it.

I hope these words help you, and even more, I hope they inspire you to be the helper your world needs.

You'd Call Me Up

I remember the year
When I needed reminders
To eat or to shower or sleep

When the days weighed a ton
And I hid from the sun
And my sadness held me in its teeth

I would wake up and stumble
Out into the kitchen
And eat just enough not to starve

Then I'd wither away
For the rest of the day
In my room in my bed in the dark

I was sure that I'd never recover
That there wasn't a thing to be done
I was sure all my good days were over
I was sure my depression had won

Then you called me up
You called every day
You said hey,
I'm just checking in,
I hope you're okay
The greatest of gifts
The simplest of love
In my lonely hour
The pain lost its power
When you called me up

I remember the season
When I lost my reason
And my manic mind took the reins
I turned into a storm
That made each day a war
In a flurry of anger and pain

When I came to myself
And I looked at the hell
That the chaos had made of my home
My werewolf went away
But my greatest fear stayed
That I would be forever alone

I was sure that I'd never recover
That there wasn't a thing to be done
I was sure all my good days were over
I was sure my mania had won

Then you called me up
You called every day
You said hey,
I'm just checking in,
I'm not going away
The greatest of gifts
The simplest of love
In my lonely hour
The pain lost its power
When you called me up

In my lonely hour
The pain lost its power
When you called me up

Minding over Mattering

Do you know the saying
Those who mind
Don't matter
And those who matter
Don't mind?

I think my problem
Is I've been minding
More than mattering.

Back To The Moon

I found myself another one
To cover up the hole
To keep out the hurt, to keep in the soul
I didn't mean to push you away
That wasn't the goal
I just didn't want to lose my control

So coffee in the morning
TV in the afternoon
Brandy in the evening
Keep my back to the moon

I never will forget the day
When I brought the stars down
I led my muse to the water
But she almost drowned
So I put her back inside me
Held my songs underneath
I smoothed out my ride
To keep her asleep

With coffee in the morning
TV in the afternoon
Brandy in the evening
Keep my back to the moon

Calliope's daughter, when she would call, I'd never reply
But then one night, accidentally
I turned my face to the sky
Billions of fires above me
Swimming in a submarine space
The dust of stars, a part of me
Wanting to find their place

Pulling in the morning
Singing in the afternoon
Aching in the evening
Drawing me back to the moon

So I took the deepest of breaths, and opened up the hole
To let in the hurt, to let out the soul
To let in the hurt, to let out the soul
To let in the hurt, to let out the soul

Cinderella

I am cleaning the floor.
On my knees.
It's not hard.

Cinderella
scrubbing her own bathroom
no paycheck in sight

What I am thinking about Is
how long we can go
Without getting on our knees

That maybe our knees hurt
Because we stand too long

I am thinking
That this floor Is better
And more beautiful
Now that I have come down
to its level
To do the work.

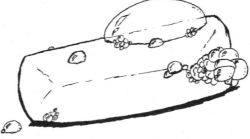

Garage Cleaning in 5 Parts

I. You

I am cleaning the garage refrigerator
Every door and possible stain
Wiping it down with soap and water
From the sink.

What I am thinking about is
my lovers
My ex-lovers.

What I am thinking about is
how many times
In intense conversation

What I thought was listening
Was really me
with a listening look
on my face

What I am thinking about is
How many times
I said "you"
When what I really meant
Was "me"

What I am thinking about
Is that perhaps
I should have said
A little more kindly,

You, you, you, you, you
You, you, you, you, you
You, you, you, you, you
You
And meant it
Every time.
What I am thinking about
Is that maybe
If I did that
I would have been ready.

II: Disarm

I am clearing out bees and other insects
That might bite or sting
From the outside of my house.

What I am thinking about is
The movies
How people
Disarm
One of two ways.

One way
Is using a weapon.
In the other way,
They put down their weapons
Raise their hands
And say, "look, no weapon"

What I am thinking about
Is which one works
The most
And which one I do
The least

III: Living

I have sprayed the moss
In my front yard.

It will take a few days time
Before it dies.
Once it does, though
It will come back
And I will have to decide
What I want to do.

Because I am not God
Or magic
I cannot make it
Disappear
Forever.

All I can do
Is what I can
Then it will do
What it does
And then it's my turn.

What I am thinking about is
That.

IV: Perfection

I am wiping the cupboards
In the garage.
No matter how hard
I press my hand
Into the wood,
Some stains
Stay put.
The point
Isn't
Complete cleanliness

The point
Of caressing
These dirty panels
Is that they will be cleaner
Then if I never touched them at all.
What I am thinking about is
I'm crying

V. Surprise

In the corner of my garage
I'm wiping the entrance down.
A red butterfly
Shocks me
From an unknown place.
It's the emptiest corner
of my garage
Totally closed off
No windows nearby.

She flickers
Towards the only opening
And disappears.

Domino's Pizza

After leaving a church in Erie, Pennsylvania where I'd been on the staff, and a failed attempt to become a Baptist missionary, I had no idea where to go or what to do.

So, I did a lot of things. I worked at the Deli counter at the local grocery store, in the garden center at Lowe's. My favorite non-music job was a children's magician. I actually continued my magic in California when I moved back – with my rabbit assistant, Cindy Lop-ear.

Then there was Domino's Pizza delivery boy. There were all sorts of interesting people working there, but one I remember the best. Her name was Lesley. She had bright red hair, a beautiful smile, and helped run the store. She rushed in and out, all the time, handling issues that were obviously far above my pay grade.

Behind a killer sense of humor and wonderful spirit, there was always a hint of something troubling going on. She never said whether it was home struggles or other trauma. But I will never forget her incredible spirit that proclaimed, "I am greater than the sum of the shadows in my life." Her focus remained on doing a good job and helping where she could. I wrote "Bigger than the Bruises" for her. I had the privilege of singing it to her personally before leaving Domino's for greener pastures.

After we know ourselves a bit, after we get a handle on our hurts, there is another stage that is necessary; to start helping. To help yourself, to help others, to be a help to the world, is one of the most identity-affirming experiences you can ever have.

This chapter is for you, Lesley; keep on shining, keep on helping. You helped me more than you may ever know.

Bigger Than The Bruises

She walks in, and you know something's up,
you just know it
But she hides it so well that you can't help but smile
She laughs because if she doesn't laugh, she'll show it
And we'll all see the tears she's been hiding a while

And when she goes back to her house at night
She tries to sleep, but her knuckles are white
And she says to no one, "I might lose this fight
Before the dawn breaks through."

But you know the night only shows the stars
It will not drown out how bright you are
Even though this world has left you scars
You're bigger than the bruises on your beautiful heart

Her pain is so great that she cries when she's sleeping
Her soul is so strong that the tears turn to pearls
Her eyes are so deep that you'd swear they were oceans
Her laugh is a spotlight that lights up the world

Do you live with the hope the hurt won't last forever?
Do you whisper a prayer by the blue of each moon?
Saying "God if you're there will you say it gets better?
Or at least will you tell me it's over soon?"

Well, you know the night only shows the stars
It will not drown out how bright you are
Even though this world has left you scars
I hear the beating of a beautiful heart
You're bigger than the bruises on your beautiful heart

I Am the Way I Can

I am the way I can forgive my brother
I am the kinder way we treat each other
I am the way I can forgive my brother
That's who I am, that's who I am

I am the way I can forgive my sister
Let go the past and tell her how I've missed her
I am the way I can forgive my sister
That's who I am, that's who I am

I am the way I can forgive my mother
I am the way I can forgive my lover
I am how clearly I can see the others
That's who I am, that's who I am

Unhungry

Here, by the sea,
i find
a creature
who eats others.

Colorful,
Spiky-mouthed,
Salty-watered,
Soft.

Does it only eat when it's hungry?
I don't know.

A piece of me
wants to believe

it only eats
when it absolutely must.

That it doesn't
sometimes
consume another
even when it is full.

A piece of me wants
to understand
a piece of me.

Now, my only thought
Is how much I have eaten
Unhungry.

Last Song

Time's moving on, I don't belong
This might be the last song from me you'll hear
Before I go, thought you should know
A few of the things in my heart I hold dear

You are a treasure, wealth is a measure
Only decided by what you believe
Go where your heart goes, all ground is hallowed
You are not shallow for chasing your dreams

Dance with the dancers, question the answers
Laugh lots of laughter, but cry lots of tears
Be who you are, right from the start,
And don't give your heart to the cancer called fear.

Talk more to strangers, they might be angels
Or broken souls God has left in your care
Some will reject you, but love will protect you
You will be better for meeting them there

Avoid pretension, shoot for redemption
Remember men are not all what they seem...
True some are devils, true some are rebels
But most are disheveled and caught in between

Dance with the dancers, question the answers
Laugh lots of laughter, but cry lots of tears...
Be who you are, right from the start,
And don't give your heart to the cancer called fear.

Alarm Clock

I wonder
What an alarm clock
Made of kindness
Sounds like?

Some questions
Don't need answers,
Only more listening

Family to Me

How long it can take
For some people to find their way
Wild Country was my first base
Took a while to find someone safe
Took a little while to open the right door
18 years, but who's keeping score?

Family, it's not the same thing to me
Not like the other ones I see
Had to leave, grow my own seeds
Find another way to plant a tree
It's not to roots that bind you,
It's the ones that set you free
And hold your wounded heart from underneath…
That's family to me

Small closet for my bed
And the feeling I'm the only one left
Light dinners, heavy times
And the feeling I'm the last of my kind
Days pass like wounds in a war
Start to wonder, who's keeping score?

Family, it's not the same thing to me
Not like the other ones I see
Had to leave, grow my own seeds
Find another way to plant a tree
It's not the roots that bind you,
It's the ones that set you free
And hold your wounded heart from underneath
That's family to me

Sometimes the weight is still heavy
Sometimes I'm all locks and no keys
But you've got a heart strong and steady
And I am so glad you're my family

The Whole Love

how many times did she put me to bed
only to be awakened, and hold me all night instead
how many transfers from booster seat to stroller
how many times my form was lifted by her shoulders

even if i add up
every motion of care
till I was two feet tall
i could never measure
the whole love of a mother at all

how many stopped escapes from gates or locks or latches
how many warnings ignored not to play with those matches
how many apologies to every babysitter
how hard i made it when she had to take me with her...

even if i add up
every single worried prayer
every bandaid for each fall
i could never measure
the whole love of a mother
at all

how many children missing mothers on this planet
how many moments have I taken mine for granted?

for every worried prayer
and every motion of care
till I was grown and tall
i will never measure
the whole love of a mother
at all

Lovers

Moulin Rouge

Moulin Rouge! arrived at just the right time and changed my life.

It was 2002. I was reeling from a suspicion that the religion I had grown up in, with its long list of codes, creeds, and do-not-do's, might not be true. Because it was ingrained in me so young and for so long, I was convinced that following its tradition was the only path for me. It was the only way to love and goodness. Anything other than that narrow way was the road to destruction. I was so protected; I didn't even know what that road looked like.

A friend of mine had a VHS of Moulin Rouge. It was most definitely not approved viewing for 16-year old good Christian boy Bobby. But we watched it anyway. I was riveted. In the flurry of noise, greed, and confusion, a simple phrase, penned by Eden Ahbez, rocked my world; "The greatest thing you'll ever learn is just to love and be loved in return."

These words rang deep inside me like a bell. Could I live by a mantra so simple?

Fast forward to 2011. I was visiting my parents for Christmas. I had recently come out to them, and a few select people. It was rough. I found myself at the edge of a decision: go to conversion therapy and bury my truth forever or embrace my sexuality and lose everything and everyone I had known up to that point. In the nostalgia of hanging Christmas lights and listening to Christmas music, there was a powerful, unspoken message hanging in the air like tinsel: "look at what you will lose if you come out."

At that moment, I made my decision. I would have one final experience in that other world, get it out of my system and then check in at "reform camp." With their help, I would bury this piece of me so far down that no one could ever find or even see it. I could keep following the rules and restore my status in this fundamentalist world.

The universe had other plans. That one final experience turned out to be John. I fell instantly in love. He was all the things I needed and had dreamed of. He was gentle, patient, loving and supportive. That love cut through all the noise and pressure. I knew this was true. "Just to love" is enough. The simple life philosophy- just to love and be loved in return - became the new foundation on which I built the rest of my life. It's served me well. My true name was coming clear.

John and I had a marvelous, loving 8 years. We began to drift apart and ultimately, decided it was best to part ways. Both of us were heartbroken.

Then, after a couple of lonely years, I met Tim. As I write this, we've been together for five years, and married for one month. He is there for me in a way few people have ever been – listening, loving, speaking the inconvenient truth when I need it, finding humor and joy in all circumstances.

Learning to love one person well has taught me more about myself and about life than any of the books I've read, the songs I've written, the sermons I've listened to. There are universal truths found in loving another - commitment, devotion, affection, communication, gentleness. I'm convinced now that loving, and being loved, is the greatest thing to learn, and that it's the solution to our overthinking, philosophizing, and all the noise we can make to distract ourselves from what is both the simplest and sometimes the hardest calling – to love one person, the one in front of us, the one offering their heart to us at this exact moment in time.

Not everyone is built for partnership. But while some are content being alone, I've found deep joy in traveling through life with someone by my side.

Opening up to love is hard. It takes faith in another person, the wildest sort of faith, one that forgives in the name of another's best self, when at times presented with their worst. Sometimes it doesn't work. Everyone's story is different. For me, love has been well worth the price of admission.

By being in love, we find one of our Truest Names – beloved.

These are my poems and songs about love in all its forms, with all its risks. That it's worth fighting for and running towards. Here's to love – may you accept it in the many ways it finds you, and share it every chance you get.

Hand on my Shoulder

Some hearts they run with the wind
Some hearts they break with a song
True what they say
Though I brushed it away,
You don't really know
What you've got
Till it's gone

Marks on the map that we pinned
Shades of the lines that we've drawn
All of the hours we gave up for our goals
Finding we wrote the poem wrong

I thought that I needed
A space to belong
I thought that I needed
A boundary line drawn
I used to be stronger
And braver
And colder
But now that I'm older
A hand on my shoulder
Will do.

Drowning

I've got my life jacket on
It's gonna be a cold one tonight
Because all the rain has come
And filled up your eyes

I've got my window rolled up
I don't want to hear it right now
But that will not keep your tears
From flooding me out

So I say what's wrong,
You say I've got to go
I say why
You say I don't quite know
But the wind has changed
And I come and squeeze your hand tight

Baby, we can't be drowning tonight
The stars are too bright
Your eyes are too beautiful
In the broken moonlight,
No we can't be drowning tonight
We're gonna make this right
our love is too wonderful to let die
So we can't be drowning tonight

Between Those Lines

There's a fire that has burned beneath my surface
There's a fire that's been burning on my mind
And its smoke signals a song
That your love is almost gone
And you don't have much to say between those lines

So I stirred up all the embers that were dying
And the sparks that flew continue still to shine
And their glow spells out a song
That my love for you is strong
And I don't have much to say between those lines

It's a world of dark and dread and fear of dying
It's amazing here that any sun could shine
But I won't give up our light
If you walk into the night
And I don't have much to say between those lines

And I will walk with you till I can go no further
Or until your hand removes itself from mine
And I will not go away
If we see some darker days
And I don't have much to say between those lines

Silver and gold won't buy me away from you
Nothing could steal away my time
From our story's bright beginning
Till one of us is through,
I will walk you every step between those lines

Come Back to Bed

You were sitting at the window when I woke up
Nothing but a bathrobe and a coffee cup
Watching the cars and the clouds move slowly
I was lying in the wrinkles and curves of your sheets
And the sun was caressing your hair and your cheeks
And I feel like I've known you for years and not weeks
And I love everything I see
Come back to bed with me

I know love's waters tend to run dry
Someday we'll have to sail through darker skies
There's always danger in unknown country
But now the night is clear and we can see the stars
And there's no creatures here to tear our hearts apart
And I will be with you, dear, until our lights grow dark
And my love, you're all I need
Come back to bed with me

This is more than the room that we're in
This is more than the touch of our skin
This is more than just two lungs breathing
This is ten thousand watts down the wire
This is my hand and your heart on fire
This is the rhythm of our hearts desire
And our bodies dance the beat
Come back to bed with me

A Hand to Hold

The night is getting darker as I wander through the trees
I can hear the wind as it rushes through the leaves
I hope it makes sense when I say I really need that sound
Cause somewhere in the silence is a voice of stone
That says I'm good for nothing and I'll never find a home
The wind is a reminder that it's going to be alright somehow

And I say, oh,
I've got a place to go
I've got a hand to hold
As the world spins around
And I,
I've got a place to hide
Now that you're by my side
Nothing's going to get me down
Cause I've got a hand to hold

The night is getting darker as I wander through the woods
If loving one another is the greatest of the goods
Why does every brother try to kick each other when they're down
Cause somewhere in the silence there's a voice of stone
That says we're good for nothing and we'll always be alone
But after I discovered you I don't believe that sound
And now we lie here in the middle of the dark
There isn't any fire but I'll still feel sparks
When you kiss me on the cheek, you make it hard to speak
You make me wanna leave the ground

And I say oh
I've got a place to go
I've got a hand to hold
As the world spins around
And I
I've got a place to hide
Now that you're by my side
Nothing's going to get me down
Cause I've got a hand to hold

Beside Me (Ryan's Song)

Every road is rough, every past is haunted
Full of small mistakes, crooked and unsure
But standing with you now
Everything I wanted
Finally has a face, finally has a cure

So wherever you are my darling
Michigan bus stop or the back of a New York car
My eyes will be the stars beside you
And wherever you run my darling
Chicago skyline or a setting Hawaiian sun
Say you'll be the one beside me

If my world goes gray, fill me up with color
If you lose your way, I'll be your place to stand
Be my sacred star, I'll be your constant cover
Tame my headstrong heart, I'll tame your heartstrong hands

So wherever you are, my darling
Michigan bus stop or the back of a New York car
My eyes will be the stars beside you
And wherever you run, my darling
Chicago skyline or a setting Hawaiian sun
Say you'll be the one beside me

Only Beloved

I have seen a thousand skies
But there is something in your eyes
I've never seen before
Like lights along the shore
Welcoming me home

And I have seen a thousand charms
But there is something in your arms
That keeps the curse at bay
It calls me by my name
Warms me to my bones

The critic in me just got fired
He's overrated
The writer in me's gotten tired
Of over-complicated

Sometimes all I wanna say
Is you're my only beloved
Of all the good things in my day,
You're the best part of it

Nice Clothes

Of all the people you could've won
Despite the craziest things that I've done
Billions of hearts beating under the sun
You chose mine

So through every problem, take me along
Set with my suns and break with my dawns,
We could go on the run
Or you could just sit on the lawn by my side

Oh, so, let me be crystal
Let me be clear
I want you with me for all of my years
So put on your nice clothes
We're going to walk down the aisle

Who could've thought there'd be stars in my night
Who could've thought love wasn't heavy, but light
Who would think worlds turned wrong into right
with a smile...

So long to sorrow, farewell to fear
With you, my darling, my doubt disappears
So put on your nice clothes,
We're going to walk down the aisle

Love doesn't need you
It won't override you
Love doesn't lead you
It lies down beside you
Once I was ready
Then love couldn't hide you
For long, now my heart, it's a song

So every December
I want you here
Holding my hand til the cold disappears
So put on your nice clothes
And we're going to walk down the aisle

Warm is the Light

I wish I could walk you through this desert storm,
You wouldn't feel dry anymore
I'd rain love on you like water, and you'd drink it up
And we'd walk hand in hand
Through the ocean of sand
And even if the sun got hotter, at least we'd be in love

But you say you'd rather be alone
That you're a one person home
And dark is the throne where your love should be
But I say there's stars in the night
There's black but there's white
And warm is the light when you're here with me

I wish I could sail you through this hurricane
Waves would storm you in vain
We'd fight violently through it towards clearer skies
And I'd steady our oars til the sand on our shore
Kissed our feet in the silence, and we'd be alive

But you say you'd rather be alone
You're a one person home
And dark is the throne where your love should be
But I say there's stars in the light
There's black but there's white
And warm is the light when you're here with me

Spark

These days roll by like thunder
But I'm still listening
Cause I've been waiting for the lightning
And it's been weeks since you crashed down on me

They say love only works out in stories
Now I'm starting to believe that it's true, but
In the morning, I have a heartbeat
Still beating strong to the bright side of you

And oh, I believe there's a spark
Somewhere hidden in your heart
And someday soon under the moon
There'll be a fire back where we started

I was so messy, when you still met me
I'd like to think I've grown
Plus I could see it, you didn't mean it
The day you let me go

And oh,
I still believe there's a spark

By My Side

Why don't you come and sit beside me
When the sun goes dark, we
Can talk till the morning comes
And when light comes knocking,
We could go out walking
Towards another setting sun

Time is of the essence
Time without your presence
Ticks along like a broken song

So if you go somewhere can I go too
Ask me anything and I'll answer true
Time just feels well spent when I walk with you
And I don't know why
Or if I leave can you come along
I'll take you to where we belong
I can feel so weak but feel strong
When you're by my side

God(s)?

Open Arms

After experiencing the fallout from being true to my queer identity, I thought it would be the last I would ever connect with, or believe in, God again. Then, when I sat down to write a song one day, I wrote about a common story in the Bible that Jesus told – the prodigal son coming home. In this story, a son returns to his father after a long time away, and the overjoyed father greets his son with open arms. I realized that through all my hurt and fear, I still somehow believed in that kind of big Love.

My faith has morphed and transformed in the following years sometimes month to month, sometimes moment to moment. But I do believe that we are held, in some way, by a love greater than our own. That deep within each of us is a clear, transcendent call to love. Atrocities happen daily, it's true – many of them carried out by individual humans – but I have also seen cases of radical forgiveness, generous love, and redemptive justice. And to me, that speaks of a greater source of love then can be carried in an individual – an Instinct or Call deep inside of us, before any of us took our first breath, beckoning us to be good. Inviting us to be kind. Daring us to choose the righteous path – not a righteousness based on piety or rule-following, but rather one where the world is better because we are in it. Our True Name, then, is a reflection of this Love that knows no bounds.

At the end of our lives, I don't know what happens. Nobody does. But if there is a God like many cultures believe, I choose to believe in One who will not be surprised by our weaknesses or mistakes, who will not be eager to punish us or condemn, but instead a Love that will greet me with open arms, a twinkle in their eye, and say "Welcome home. I'm glad you're here."

Still in Love

Drawn away like sailors to the sea,
Pulled away from shore to find some peace
Since I've sailed away I'm not the same
But still across the waves I hear my name

Less is more is what you always say
But I want more and so I run away
I feel worse with every choice I choose
And I know that your heart is breaking too

But I'm still in love with you, God
I'm still in love with you
I could deny that affection
With everything I do
But I'm still in love with you

Lonely is my heart and full of fear
Lonely is the road that brought me here
Lonelier the farther on I go
But I'm afraid to start the long walk home

My feet drag and stumble down the track
Heavy are the burdens on my back
I cry as I see you start to run
I'm not worthy to be called your son

But you're still in love with me, God
You're still in love with me
And I can feel it in the warm embrace
The robe, the ring, the feast that
You're still in love with me

And I'm still in love with you, God
I'm still in love with you
And when I start to wander, remind me of this truth,
That I'm still in love with you

And you're still in love with me

Most Days

Sometimes I feel like you're a meddlesome Mother
And I'm pushing up against your will
Sometimes I feel like you're a prodigal Father
Like you're gone, and I'm here
Wondering if you love me still

I'm trying to find the faith
But I'd much prefer the proof
And I'm standing in the space between the two

So I hold onto you when I can't find the way
So I hold onto you most days
I hold onto you when I don't know what to say
So I hold onto you most days

Sometimes I feel like you're a wide open clearing
And you're going to catch me
No matter if or when I fall, but
Sometimes I feel like you are so hard of hearing
That I speak your name for days
And wind up wondering if you're there at all

When I've drunk up all my wine, but I've still got all this time
When my whole body feels fine, but something's bleeding
When I've always done my part, but I still have all these scars
When the life I love feels far from the life I'm leading

That's when I hold onto you
So I hold onto you Most Days

Save What You Can

It's so dark inside this shell
Don't remember when I fell
Feels like the walls are caving in
Feels like I'm back where I begin
But that's alright
Save what you can from my life

I am not immune to pain
I am not immune to stains
Feels like I'm broken past repair
Feels like the trade would be unfair
But that's alright
Save what you can from my life

The way you see right through me
The way you see right through my eyes
The way you look into me
The way you look into my life
Feels like you're taking out what's fake
Feels like the dawn's about to break
And that's just right
Save what you can from my life

Another Pulse

Rise with the sun, then follow it down
Try to embrace the shadow
Ear to the floor, head to the ground
Hear from the earth an echo

You came from me, boy
Dust of my dust
And one day, when we're ready
You'll return to us

Past all my needs
Roots of the trees
Drink from a sea beneath me
Though I've been blind
Cruel and unkind
Still the earth's voice, it greets me

You came from me, boy
Dust of my dust
And one day, when we're ready
You'll return to us
And after you feel you've done all you can do
I carry the seas, I can carry you

Tornado mind, rushing through time
Coffee to wine to lover
Then back to the trees, grass under feet
Feel underneath another pulse

You came from me, boy
Dust of my dust
And one day, when we're ready
You'll return to us
And when you've made plans but they've all fallen through
I grew all the trees, i can grow you too, I can grow you too

Oh, i have felt it
Beating inside me
The tectonic, powerful heart of the earth
It shoulders and carries
Grows what gets buried
Present for every birth
So when I am empty
And dark is the day
Up from the ground, I hear sounds
I wish father would say
I wish mother would say

You came from me, boy
Leaf of my leaf
And when you fall over,
I am always underneath

Lion in the Summer

Answers don't come easy
Like they used to, like they did when I was seventeen
And if it's this bad now
I wonder what it's gonna be like when I'm sixty-three

The minute hand keeps moving and I can't escape its sound
We're falling down an hourglass that never turns around

My spirit leaves me and I don't know where it goes
Feels like I do the same things over and over
If Jesus comes for me, I don't think that I'll ever be prepared
And I'm like a lion in the summer
But every other season I'm just scared

I shook my fist at God
But still that didn't stop the angels watching over me
I tried to lose my faith
But I just can't escape the feeling someone's holding me

And if there's someone up there
Then I hope I make them proud, but
Most days I do best
If I just keep my demons down

Out on the water I feel healthy and sane
I hear my sons and daughters calling my name
I've never seen them, but I know just the same
They're there.

I've got these fears and they're tied straight to my chest
I've got these dreams and no idea what's best, but
I see the waves and hear them tell me to rest
There, there.

And I'm like a lion in the summer
But every other season I'm just scared

Ever Since

Ever since I was a little boy
I believed in something good.
And so I did my best to go to Sunday school,
Every Sunday like I should

And I remember the day when I had to leave
And I thought it was all a stage
I let fear and anger get hold on me
And they locked me in their cage

But when love came creeping through the window pane
All I could do was wonder why
I swore I did not deserve it but still it came,
And now it holds me when I cry

And ever since I was a little boy
I believed in something good

Luck might be a Lady

When you started out to get to where you're at
Did you spin a wheel or did you check a map
Did you do some preparation, or only by inspiration
And just hope the Holy Ghost would fill the gaps

When you left the place you were for where you are
Did you take some time to pick your plan apart
Or instead, did you just wing it,
Take your can of paint and fling it
counting every single stain a work of art

Luck might be a lady, she'll help a few times maybe
But she didn't write your pattern in the stars
Luck might be a lady
But fate is the woman in charge

In a bright casino full of frantic sin
All the neon says you probably will win
So you fling your money at it, and you pray to some old magic
And the dealer says, you better go all in

Luck might be a lady, she'll help a few times maybe
But she didn't write your pattern in the stars
Luck might be a lady
But fate is the woman in charge

Maybe Stars

I know you're too old to believe in fairy tales
You've made mistakes you've had tough breaks
And most your plans have failed
I know that faith is just as strong as what it's in
And you tried God and They were not what you expected and
So you gave it up and left it all behind
But maybe stars will change your mind

I know control is something that's hard to give up
People are fools and can be cruel and most are hard to trust
I know that you have had your full of phony stuff
And you have spent up every cent and still feel out of love
So you decided truth was hard to find
But maybe stars can change your mind

So come take a walk with me across the galaxy
10 million miles away into the mystery
Maybe there's wonder there that everybody shares
And if you think the Universe is blind
Maybe stars will change your mind

I know you're too old to believe in fairy tales
But maybe stars

How long I will pray

Until my anxious head stops its worry
That's how long I will pray
Until my heavy heart stops its hurry
That's how long I will pray

Until I hear the sacred in the silence
That's how long I will pray
Until I feel an end to inner violence
That's how long I will pray

Until I hear my maker's calmer calling
That's how long I will pray
Until I feel my inhibitions falling
That's how long I will pray

Until my time condenses to this moment
That's how long I will pray
Until I feel no more need for atonement
That's how long I will pray

Carry Me Away

Oh, my fearful heart
They say it's safe here, but
It gets so hard sometimes
I need a brand new start
Out past these city streets
Beyond their borderlines

I fought my demons down
And when they finally fell
Oh what a graceful sound
You saw me through the crowd
You came and found me, and
You wrapped around me

And oh, my love
Carry me away, Carry me away

Oh, my unclean hands
Where have you been, at least
Tell me these wounds are mine
I need a brand new plan
One where before I leap
At least I look inside

I tried to fill my cup
With such ambition that
It almost drank me, but
It all comes down to love
It came and found me and
It wrapped around me

And oh, my love
Carry me away
Carry me away

O Little Town

These days I'm not at peace
These days I hardly sleep
These days I'm lost between
What should've been and what might be.
I want some certainty
I want a guarantee
I want a good plan B
Before I say yes to the Mystery.

O little town turned upside down
Looking for clearer signs
Above our soul's fight for control
The stars seem unsurprised
And could there be in these dark streets
An ever-lasting light
Could hopes and fears of all my years
find rest in me tonight

These days I search for peace
In faces that I see
Wondering what's underneath
Do they want to love or leave me
I need a signed release
Before I feel set free
Permission slip to be
Before I feel I'm worthy

O little town
With hearts so bound
How hard we toil and try
Above our deep
And doubting sleep
The stars seem satisfied

Oh, could it be
The peace we seek
Has already arrived
Where hopes and fears of all the years
Find rest in me tonight

These days I think of peace
Just like I think of trust
Is it a fantasy
Or a real gift waiting for us?
We dream of well-sealed doors
We dream of lasting safety
Instead, the Christmas story
Tells us Love comes like a baby

Oh little town
With souls locked down
So much to hold and hide
Above our sleep
The canopy
The stars seems satisfied
Oh, could it be
The peace we need
Has already arrived
The hopes and fears of all our years
Find rest in me tonight

The Spellcaster Says

The Spellcaster Says
There isn't really a secret
Just things you're afraid of knowing

The Spellcaster Says
You'll know the spell is working
When the spell is working
on you.

The Spellcaster Says
Yes, of course love is the answer
Your need for spells is the question

The Spellcaster Says
The hurt in your heart can be helped
But some feathers and clay won't do
You'll need to bring your own open heart
To the ceremony

The Spellcaster Says
Jesus was one of the best Spellcasters
But, he said we would cast bigger spells
We keep looking at him to measure ours
He would wonder why
Our spells try to mirror the old
When he specifically asked for all things new

The Spellcaster Says
Be not afraid
And I remember hearing that
Somewhere else

Here

I'm Okay

My childhood culture was obsessed with the afterlife. We believed in a "rapture" of the saints, where the good people would be taken by Jesus one day to heaven in the blink of an eye, and the bad eggs – those who hadn't prayed the sinner's prayer or who hadn't meant their prayer enough – would be left behind. Sometimes, as a child, when my parents took the dog for a walk and would be away too long, I panicked, certain they had been taken.

We were taught that everything here was in preparation for what would happen after we died. Because of this, I found myself always struggling with a childhood fear of "Am I doing enough? Do I have enough to make it? Is there something missing in my life or am I checking all the boxes?" No matter how many times I prayed the prayer, I never knew if I meant it enough.

This is an exhausting way to live, forever double-checking our list of what we are doing in the present in light of the future after death. I found myself carrying it with me, even after leaving that culture… wondering constantly if I would be okay.

For years after, my mantra of comfort to combat this bone-deep, childhood fear was "you're going to be okay." But one day, a counselor heard me say this, and they said "What about a mantra that says 'I'm okay right now. What would that feel like?'" That idea had never even occurred for me.

Since then, I've completely changed my perspective. Instead of working towards a future where I'll be okay, I've asked myself what it would look like to believe I have and am enough, right now. In this precious present moment, looking around and saying "This is peace, right here. This is good, right here. I'm okay, right now."

By the way, living all those years in Northern California, we live with small earthquakes and tremors. Even now, when awakened in the night by a sound, my first thought is sometimes "He's here!" The fear of missing the rapture runs deep! But I'm okay. Right now.

Outer Space

Unknown and unproven
Yet we trace our future there
Astrology, horoscopes, divination

So much easier
Looking far away for answers
Then to put the telescope down

Breathe in up-close air
Take in reachable space
Observe countable time

And say "I'll start here"

Abundance

The door is a window to a million good things
Locked with a heart-shaped lock.
and all my keys are wrong-shaped

I jangle,
pushing them against wrong openings
looking, tiring with force

There isn't a lovely ending to this.
The door opens from the inside.

Someday,
I will settle into my body.

Someday,
I will settle into my beauty.

Someday.

Trading In

I'm trading deadlines for a softer ceiling
I'm trading lonely for a truer feeling
I'm trading easy for a harder healing
But one that leaves me whole

I'm trading running for a hand beside me
Trading my shadows for a light that won't hide me
Traded my money for a love it won't buy me
And a little less control

And we pick up so much when we're living
that we should never hold
We carry so much we should never own

But all that I need is what I've been given
Right inside this skin
Everything else that doesn't treat me well
I'm trading in, I'm trading in

I'm trading safety the world has sold me
For something wilder and real and holy
For what the ghost of my father told me
That you're already home
Anywhere you go

And all that I need I've already been given
Right inside this skin
Everything else that doesn't treat me well
I'm trading in, I'm trading in

The Tribeless Tribe

You are not abnormal, different,
Unusually shattered
by life's hammer hand.

You share the same fragmented
pieces of confusion and beauty,
Love and anger,
war and peace,
As most of us misfits.

If we didn't, we would lose
The casual kindness
Of someone who's survived.

We would lose sight of the fact
That we are all part of
The largest family;
The tribeless tribe.

Ready to Be Found

I know where the lost ones go
When they spend too much time out on the open road
They flicker in and out of life like ghosts
You can see through their feet to the ground
I know 'cause I've been one of them
Lately as last year, no time for friends
I can create a thousand loose ends
and never even bother to count
But I'm ready for that to change now,
I'm ready for that to change

I think it's time to let my wanderlust rest
Lay my head on a forgiving chest
Close my eyes and listen to a warm, steady sound
And I'm not saying it's the end
Just think it's time I made room for a friend
Some things in me won't grow without roots in the ground
I think I'm ready to be found

I've spent so much of my life as a seeker
Standing still burns like a fever
My sense of home in my soul has gotten weaker
But I'm ready to turn it around
I think I'm ready to be found

Once I was walking alone, after too many nights on the road
I looked down, and what do you know
I could see through my feet to the ground
I think I'm ready to be found.

Home In Your Body

Oh,
You'll never love anyone else right
Until you have love for yourself

Know,
Until you're at home in your body
You won't be home anywhere else

Planetarium

Our car parks, and I
Crawl out of the backseat
And into the breezy evening.

My parents walk behind me
As I dash ahead, looking for
Anything to pay attention to.

Walking through the doors
Of the lobby, I find a meteorite
Dark, textured, wondrous, old.

Inside, our seats lean back
And a dome above us slowly
Starts to light up with pinpricks.

The narrator leads us along
Constellations and atmospheres
Black holes and comets and supernovas.

To be here
Amidst vast whirlpools of gas and fire
To be here, in this chair, on this Earth.

The presentation ends with the sun
Slowly pouring its light onto the dome
Making the stars fade and then disappear.

Walking out into the windy night
I am always quiet, full of thoughts
And deeper than thoughts, a feeling.

It's one I carry with me now
And revisit when days are hard
Or life pulls me under its weight

A feeling, that of all the dots of light,
In all the galaxies in all the universe
The wonder, the wonder, to be here.

Never For Sale

The buyers who've owned you
And those who've disowned you
Let their loans default and fail
You were never up for sale
You were never up for sale

Let there Be Dark

In my bible
As a 7 year old
I would turn the pages
To genesis
And it said
Darkness
Was on the face of the deep.
Then the light came.

I am wondering about darkness
If we allow it
Inside our own convictions
and comfort and convenience.

If we don't,
Life just becomes
Blindingly bright.

So I think
Let there be dark.
The stars need a stage
And I need to let go of
My own prideful knowing a bit,
I think
Before this light of mine
Can be truly true

Ungrateful

Fire and waves and forests
Cinnamon and wind
Pain and hope and wonder
Trapped inside these bones and skin
Beauty all around me
That I never stop to find
I can be so ungrateful sometimes

I hurricane through hours
With a hundred things to do
Craving these few moments
When the only thing is you
But then a bright screen calls me
And I leave you with the wine`
I can be so ungrateful sometimes

Finally make it back
From all the songs and shows and sparks
And you are home from work
And watching TV in the dark
Stumble through the doorway
After tour for weeks and weeks
Drop my heavy suitcase
Kiss your hands, your mouth your cheeks
And the moon's a golden beacon on the ocean of your eyes
I can be so ungrateful sometimes

But, sometimes...

I Cleaned My Car Today

I cleaned my car today
It's a thing I had to do
It was overstuffed with little things
And memories of you
I had nowhere left to run
I had nothing left to say
So I let the sadness come
And cleaned my car today

I cleaned my car today
It was more than about time
I'd been waiting for a moment
When I had a clearer mind
When I had a clearer heart
And was in a better space
But that moment seemed too far
So I cleaned my car today

I cleaned my car today
Using everything I knew
And the dust mites sang the hallelujah
Chorus as they flew
And the trash jumped in its bag
And the stains all rubbed away
And I found some peace at last
When I cleaned my car today

"You are going to be okay"
Spoke a voice so kind and clear
And it came from somewhere else
Because you certainly weren't here
"You are going to be okay"
From above and underneath
And it was so strong and certain
That it couldn't have been me

You don't love a chapter less
Because you have to turn the page
I still love you, you're the best
And dear, I cleaned my car today.

We Don't Own Anything At All

We don't own anything at all
It's just a loan
From Father Time and Mother Space
Can't own a person, thing, or place
Even your tears after they fall
We don't own anything at all

Time

Time Traveller

"Time will tell, she'll see us through."
-Gregory Alan Isakov

I've always been fascinated and moved by the passage of time. I remember at five or six years old, suddenly realizing that one day I'd go to college and be away from my parents. I burst into tears. Suddenly, I felt distinctly in two different times – the present moment where I was with my mom and dad, and a future where I wasn't – and even though it hadn't happened yet, somehow the future was happening right in that moment. My poor parents!

Growing older, I have less moments where I time-travel into the future, and much more where I find myself transported to the past. A song comes on, and I find myself deep in emotion with the memories of a place, or a deep love. I'm so thankful when that happens, and instead of judging myself for 'losing' the moment, I give it its due, and feel it out, before moving on with my day.

Time can fly by, or crawl, depending on the circumstance – but one sure thing, as true as gravity, is time always marches us forward. That certainty puts an urgency on this moment, and instead of anxiety, I like to allow it to give me a sense that what I'm doing now can hold deep meaning. Whether or not we keep time, time keeps us in its constant, steady flow, and when I swim with its current, not in denial of it, my days and moments always bloom brighter.

Somedays

No cars or friends to meet
Waves crashing at my feet
I've left my troubles far behind
On the sidewalk of main street
The sea is broken glass
The sun is fading fast
So I will drink the waves I see
'Cause I can't take them home with me

But someday, I will walk away
Someday I'll be free
And I'll leave my cellphone on the bay
Sail across the waves towards the place where the
Horizon meets the sea
But someday's running out on me,
My somedays are running out on me

My schedule's overbooked
My heart's been overlooked
I've traded in my hopes and dreams for
Social securities
I want a better way
I want a bigger say
In how I live my dying days
I want to choose who I obey

Someday, I will walk away
But my Somedays are running out on me

I'm tired of crawling out of bed,
Without a reason to breathe
I'm tired of wishing what I said
Was something I believed enough
To try to be

But someday's running out on me
The hourglass is drowning me
Sand is crashing down on me
My somedays are running out on me

The River

Today, the river
Entered my eyes and ears
Wound its way through
Flesh, spirit, bone

Using liquid strength and sound
To gently smooth out
Tin-foil wrinkles
Of worry and weight
Business and busy-ness

Until finally, I remembered
How much water I'm made of,
How many drops I have left,
And how little time I have
To drink.

Most Good Things Take Time

When I was five years old, I couldn't grow a garden
Watered way too hard
I wasn't good at reading the signs

And as the days would pass
 I would watch the plants grow
String beans and tomatoes
I'd pick them both as soon as they appeared on the vine

It took a while to learn
That most good things take time

When I was 17, I was always in a hurry
Still always late, head filled with worry
So much on my plate but never stopping to taste
And I convinced myself that taking any break was a waste

It took a while to learn it, a lot of bridges burning
A lot of hourglasses turned before their prime
Until I finally found out,
taking time is a good thing
And most good things take time

When I was twenty-three, I started writing music, had to heal some wounds
next thing I knew, the song was my life
Now I'm thirty-seven, fourteen years later
and I watch some friends take the elevator
While I climb these stairs late into the night
And I wish them well, I really hope they make it
But from what I see, most elevators break
And meanwhile, my legs are getting strong from this climb
'Cause taking time is a good thing
And most good things take time

When I was 5 years old, I couldn't grow a garden
But now, I just might try

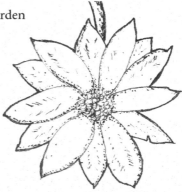

Everybody's Leaving

Climb the stairs to my grandfather's home
Don't know who you are at 12 years old
How the faces look, like a half closed book
Quiet and kind and a little cold
See his body past the bedroom door
Hear them say he's not there anymore
Watch his face awhile, hope to see him smile
Hope to see a wave crash upon his shore

Hug all the extended family,
Never seen the end of anything,
See his face again as you go to leave
Realize the truth in the back seat

Everybody's leaving, even if they're leaving slow
Dancing towards the light, trying to get it right
Hoping that our lifeline holds
Every breath you're breathing
Its value is more than any gold
It's funny isn't it, our most important gift
Is something we can never hold

Byron gets a job at the supermarket
Cathy takes the phones from nine to five
And if anybody asks them how they're doing
They say they're doing fine, fine, fine
But Byron has a recurring dream every night
Of living in a cabin under stars
And Cathy dreams of wild, wild horses
Far away from cities and cable cars
Is their life too full, no vacancy
Have they seen the end of anything
How long till the lock doesn't take a key
And they lose their chance at being free

Cause everybody's leaving
Even if they're leaving slow
We're all dancing in the dark
Trying to make our mark
Hoping that our lifeline holds
So every breath you're breathing
Hope you know it's worth more than any gold

117

My Best Song

I hope I write my best song at a hundred and one
I hope that it blows out the water
Anything else that I've ever done
I hope it sounds better than I've ever sung
My best song at a hundred and one

I hope I kiss my best kiss at a hundred and three
I hope that it makes you blush, whoever's in front of me
I hope it means as much as a kiss could ever mean
My best kiss at a hundred and three

And as the world keeps turning, hope I never stop learning
Long as my light keeps burning, hope I never stop learning
I'll write my best song at a hundred and one

I hope I dream my best dream at a hundred and four
I hope it's full of light and color
Wide oceans and endless shores
I hope it feels real, and good at its core
I hope I dream my best dream at a hundred and four

And as the world keeps turning, hope I never stop learning
Long as my light keeps burning, hope I never stop learning
My best dream at a hundred and four

Sing Along

From the place where I now lay my shadow
To my childhood home on Santa Barbara Drive
Although I'm ashamed to say it
I'll admit that I have not yet found my tribe

When the winds of life start hurricanes
There's barely even time to touch the ground
There's so much beauty, so much pain
But I'm learning not to separate the sounds
So I stretch my crimson cord out, reaching for a distant shore
Where everything's okay and nothing's aching
But it's a long way across Jordan
There are boats, I can't afford them
So I'll float to where the current takes me

And sing along, let it go
It's not easy I know
But life's a gift, then it goes, then it's gone
So sing along

The heart can be a painful dancer
It's much easier to let it turn to stone
And I don't have many answers
I just know that I don't wanna be alone

So singalong, let me in
We are more than just skin
We are soul, fire and wind
Together strong
Love, we all tend to rust
We are children of dust
But you are here, and life is short, and love's the song
So sing along

As my song bleeds out with each midnight sky
Let my love run deep, let my hate run dry
They say that some things never die
They go on and on and on and on

Oh sing along, let it go
We are all headed home

Worthy

If I die tonight
I will see you in the morning
If I die tonight
There will be another day
On the grass outside
Drops of morning dew will gather
And the sun will come
As if nothing had gone away

And all the trees will clap their hands
And the rocks will understand
Worthy is the lamb

If I die tonight
There will be another summer
And there will be a fall
And there will be a winter snow
And as the darkness fades
Ice will wander down the rivers
And then when spring is here
Rain will make the flowers grow

And I'm a broken soul
And futile words are on my tongue
And I can't sing to you
What someone greater has not sung

And all the trees will clap their hands
And the rocks will understand
Worthy is the lamb, worthy is the lamb

Dear December

Dear December, your gray skies
Didn't see them in April's eyes
She was all hopes and good daydreams
Now it's darker, help me see the
Point of waiting, point of standing still
Point of opening up to the chill
Point of losing, and letting go
The point of choosing to let your heart come home

Dear December, End of Years
Rest in peace, all you hopes and fears
Beneath chimneys, embers glow
Smell of cider, mistletoe
Now it's colder, now I'm older
Now I'm fuller grown
Now I'm trying to let my heart come home

We the lovers, we the friends
We the holders of hundreds of loose ends
We who stumble, we who fall
Dear December, you hold us all
We too busy to sing our songs
We who've wandered for far too long
While we're waiting, while we're standing still
Taking time for our empty to refill
Dear December, so you know
I am letting my heavy heart come home

In The Middle Of the Question

When life gets complicated
when life gets hard to understand

The simple things grow sacred
like the touch of another hand

Everything underrated
everything buried underneath

In the present gets appreciated
when the future is a mystery

So I'm not bringing any answers
and I'm not sure if there's a lesson

But we can walk through this together
and love each other through the question

And there may never be an answer
On this side of the lesson

But I believe that Love walks with us
in the middle of the question

There Is A Shore

These days, I love more than statues the dancers
These days, I love more the questions then answers
Like, how does a moon look so good over a shore?
And why, when I see it, I don't feel alone anymore

I've wandered far, over the hillsides
Under the stars, between the headlights
Up on the cliffs, down through the valleys below
I'm looking for final atonement
Joy for the mind, peace for each moment
Not just the ones between start and end of a show

I've been brought to my knees, fighting for peace
Oh what a war
Though there's none I can see, still I believe
There is a shore

One day you wake up and ask where the care went
One day you find out no permanent parent
One day, you find out, even the best things can end
But still, I believe, though the signal is weaker
And years have placed static between Sound and Speaker
Still I can hear the Song of a forever friend
I hope I find It again

Last night I dreamt of a forgotten town
All my lost memories dancing around
And God, she showed up
In a gossamer gown
She lifted my head up as I looked down
She lifted my head up and said

You've been brought to your knees, Fighting for peace
Oh, what a storm inside you
Though it's hard to believe, Deep underneath
There is a shore inside you. I've placed a shore inside you.

Verbs

Nouns Need Verbs

In my song "Wild, Wild Heart" has a line:

You have got a wild, wild heart
doesn't need a home
time to let it go

Here's why I don't believe the heart needs a home: I believe the heart is a home, in and of itself. We can find all sorts of temporary places to belong – a house, a community, a person – but ultimately, one of the best truths of life is that "home is where the heart is" and your heart is always with you, whether you remember it or not. A feeling of belonging can exist just by the fact that we are alive, on this incredible planet, in this amazing time. And, if we believe our hearts are home enough, then we can stop spending energy finding another place, and spend it in courageous, good action. This is why I'm so committed to the idea of our True Name. Once we believe that, we can stop searching for the perfect noun to define us, and lean into the beautiful world of verbs.

I think a lot of our resentment that builds up against people, places, and things comes from the false idea that something will fulfill or fix us in a way that only our own hearts can do. Expecting a partner to be everything for us that we are supposed to be for ourselves. Rejecting a community because they don't live up to our ideal. Becoming disappointed in an object that we purchased because the void is still there.

I know this may be a controversial opinion, but I don't believe there is a void at the heart of life. I believe that the void is created when we stifle or ignore our own soul's call to be at home in itself, and to live an openhearted life in line with our true identity.

All that to say, I believe our hearts were made for motion. Our nouns need verbs to have life. We can say what we believe our True Name is all we want – but until we start acting on our Name, people will never know what our true nature is. Nouns are great for stability and personal identity, but it's the verbs of life that truly define us to the people around us.

Once we believe our hearts are the only home we'll ever need, we can let them go and become the wild, wonderful, surprising, active spirits we were meant to be. We can start to live a life that is in motion instead of in stasis, unable to leave the nest or open the cage. We can become a force of good in the world. So, in a world currently pursuing meditation and standing still as a means of spiritual enlightenment, I want to also raise a glass to the verbs of our lives – the actions of our wild hearts, that help ourselves be love to the world and the beautiful people in it.

Wild, Wild Heart

So if you think that staying here will keep you safe it won't
So stumble from the creek of what you think you know
to the sea of what you don't
Sometimes the nest becomes a cage
And what you need is right outside the dome

You have got a wild, wild heart
Time to let it go, go, go

It's never wise to run away
Since we were little kids, always the race to be safe
It's fine to try and run the plates
So long as the final stop is home base
But sometimes the nest becomes a cage
And you have got a wild, wild heart

You have got a wild, wild heart
Doesn't need a home, time to let it go
You have got a wild, wild heart
Time to let it go, go, go

No Container

Even in a small container
With an opening
Gardens can grow

But just wait; one day
We will open the lid
Of our limits

And discover
What can happen
Beyond the glass walls
Of over-carefulness

Something You Happen To

december 31st, pull up the shiny hearse
put in the old year, break the reverse gear
the past pulls out your driveway, forever out of reach

oh what a sunset, don't know how many left
time is a treasure chest only spent never kept
turn down the fear of failing, and set your life story free
I know it's easy to give up
With everything you've been through, but
life isn't just what happens
it's something you happen to

the future is a highway
growing beneath our feet
forever incomplete
always awakening
so let go all the dark things
that have been done to you
life isn't just what happens
it's something you happen to

so let the new year grow, take it sure and slow
never look back except to learn or laugh
wounds are our greatest teachers, scars are our strangest strength
hold your hurt hand high, wave a good goodbye
the dawn only breaks after the old day dies
time moves us ever forward into the mystery
and every moment changes based on the way we move
life isn't just what happens...it's something you happen to

the future is a highway
growing beneath our feet
forever incomplete
always awakening
so let go all the dark things
that have been done to you
life isn't just what happens
it's something you happen to

Flip The Tassel

Sometimes to graduate
You need to cross the lawn
Climb the stairs
Flip the tassel
And move along

It's not that you are better
You've just heard a stronger song
So climb the stairs
Flip the tassel
And move along

Wave goodbye to those who linger
On the safe side of the lawn
Climb the stairs
Flip the tassel
And move along

Before the End

We walk, we walk on eggshells til we fall
We don't give much until we lose it all
We hear, we hear the greener pastures call
But our fear is too big and our hearts to small

This is not a test, this is your life
One chance to live best, this is the right time
Tomorrow you'll have less of it to spend
After this moment's past, there's no refund
This breath could be your last, make it a good one
Love is the best thing you can give, my friend
Before the end

We know, we know the truth will set us free
But we run, we run away because we're scared to see ourselves
And we want the resurrection without the calvary
The thrill of the jump without the fear of falling
Oh, if we could see past the dark
If we could see fire before we had to spark
If could know who we are
Before we had to be it,
Wouldn't it be wonderful but

This is not a test, this is your life
One chance to live best, this is the right time
Tomorrow you'll have less of it to spend
After this moment's past, there's no refund
This breath could be your last, make it a good one
Love is the best thing you can give, my friend
Before the end

Color Mine

You can keep life black and white
I'm going to color mine
You can hold your reins in tight
I'm going to jump the lines
You can keep your shore in sight
My ship has waves to climb
You can monochrome your life
I'm going to color mine.

When Your Dream Wakes Up

I have seen it, seen it for myself
When a dream wakes up and finds its lover come home
I have been there, on that hallowed ground
Heard those sacred sounds
So don't leave your dream alone

Doubt the dark pretender, faith the fierce defender
I feel them fighting over me
So I build the ordinary round me like a sanctuary
I've heard that all good dreams have teeth
And it's okay if you're scared
We're all afraid we're not enough
But just make sure that you're there
When your dream wakes up

Some are savers for a later time
When their world unwinds
And all their worries fade
But nothing's certain, final curtain call
Is different for us all
So don't hide you dream away

Pain the cold commander, love the only answer
I feel them fighting over me
So I build the ordinary round me like a sanctuary
I've heard that all good dreams have teeth
And it's okay that you're scared
Most of us think we're not enough
But just make sure that you're there
when your dream wakes up

The Ancient Portal

I looked through
An ancient portal
Saw the invitation
To a new reality
Stepped close
Took a picture
To show my friends
And kept walking

Bon Voyage

An open hearted journey's calling me
So good I feel it must be make believe
It's just too beautiful
I didn't know life could stay beautiful
I'm used to living on the edge of me
I'm used to keeping my hopes underneath
Try not to lose control, keep my ambition tame and dutiful

But there's an open road to bluer skies now
There's an invitation to surprise now
There's a happiness that stays inside now
And doesn't stop, it doesn't stop
So I'm leaving smaller dreams behind now
Bon voyage

Been waiting tables for the kings
Settling for ordinary things
Towing the easy line, saying thanks I'm fine
Oh, but not this time, no not this time

'Cause there's a rainbow's end before my sight now
I can see the world with wider eyes now
My heart's being pulled by stronger tides now
And they won't stop, no they won't stop
So I'm leaving smaller dreams behind now
Bon Voyage.

Nothing In the Way

You've got an open runway
I hope mine clears someday
But right now there's too much
Between me and the sky
You've got two wings and a steady pace
But I've got a chain around my waist
That only I can untie
Can you let me go softly
And try not to say never
Can you take your heart off me
And hope it's not forever

And I know that, though it hurts bad
I'm going to need some time
And I don't want to fight
There's nothing left to say
But when I come back, when I come back
I'm going to love you right
With nothing in the way

And I know it's unfair of me
But I hope you're still going to love me
After I go away
And do the wilder things that I gotta do
You've got a master's degree in trust
I've got a wall to make Jericho blush
That only I can break through

And I know that, to get my soul back
I'm going to need some time
And I don't want to fight
There's nothing left to say
But when I come back, when I come back
I'm going to love you right
With nothing in the way

This Year, I Learned

This year I learned what it means to be true
at the cost of comfortable
This year, I learned things I think are concrete
can still be combustible

And as we wait for the dawn
Time it marches on, The Eternal Advancer
But in the eyes of my friends
I think I see it again, the edge of an answer

This year, I learned to help the tables turn
You gotta love someone you don't need any reasons
And we're battle-scarred but that's not all we are
Lift up your eyes and see the forest through the treasons

This year, I learned sometimes a fire burns
And you don't get to say when or how long, or how high or why
You've just gotta take a breath
make a decision on what to do with what's next
And hold up your loves til the tears run dry
And as we wait for the dawn,
time it marches on, the eternal advancer
But when I turn to what's left
I feel in every breath the edge of an answer

This year, I learned to help the tables turn
You gotta love someone you don't need any reasons
And we're battle-scarred but that's not all we are
Lift up your eyes and see the forest through the treasons

Edge Of The World

At the edge of the world, when it seems like you might fall
That's when you face the choice
to go back to the middle of it all
Or be brave, and jump off

The million acre land of things we cannot see
So hard to make a plan
when even the mirror's a mystery

So we make decisions on demand
and then make revisions every scene
The future's in your hands
You get to choose your destiny
As if it's easy, writing a story
without knowing the ending

There's an edge to every world
and it can make us feel so scared
But that's when we face the choice to go back
To where no one really cares
Or be brave, and jump off

And we're not afraid to die, my dear
No I don't think that's why we're torn
Let's look the mirror in its eyes, my dear
Find out we're scared of being born
At the edge of the world

Just One More

there was a sound that I found

at the bottom of everything

there was a noise, not a voice

but the sound of someone

holding me

Acknowledgements

To all the people who have heard these lyrics and read this poetry and said "you should turn these into a book." To all who have believed in me. My thanks to you is immeasurable.

To my first children's librarian, who softly guided me towards books that made me fall in love with words. You may never know how far your gift has spread, but I do.

To my Mom, Joy and my Dad, Jim, for choosing me.

To John, who taught me to love first; to Sabrina and Josh, who taught me to love fiercely; and to Tim, who taught me to love and believe in myself (I'm still learning, darling).

To Kathi, Jim, Neil, who all took the time to read this in advance and offer their kind words in support of this collection.

To you, for spending your time with these pieces of me. If you like this, if this helped in any way, please pass it along or grab a copy for a friend you think would love it. Thank you.

Biography

Bobby Jo Valentine's music exists outside the lines of any genre, but the music's thoughtful, spirit focused lyrics and catchy melodies reach listeners across all walks of life. The poetic nature and spiritual focus of his stories and songs has resulted in notable awards and a growing, loyal following around the country. He's found a voice with original, hopeful songs about the gentle everyday spiritual awakenings of an openhearted life.

Growing up and emerging out of a Baptist Church of strict lines and sharp edges, Bobby Jo Valentine has emerged into a larger, kinder, more welcoming faith...one that is excited to learn, open to growth, and focused on love.

Along with theaters, house concerts, and many other kinds of stages, Bobby is often invited to offer his stories and songs at faith communities around the nation. Among others, he has been invited to perform for The Wild Goose Festival, the international Emerge Conference, and the 2017 General Synod of the United Church of Christ. His music has won Song of the Year twice at West Coast Songwriters Association, and his work has appeared on radio, TV, and feature films. He has performed artist residencies, hosted songwriting workshops, and been involved in helping communities of all types use their spaces and voice in more creative and powerful ways.

Bobby currently hails from Portland, OR where he lives with his husband, Tim, and their puppy, Tater Tot.

You can hear music, watch performances, and get information on catching a show at www.bobbyjovalentine.com